Triptych

By the same author:

# Triptych:

## Collected Works Volume 7

# John Watson

PUNCHER & WATTMANN

First published in 2018
Published by Puncher and Wattmann
PO Box 441
Glebe NSW 2037

http://www.puncherandwattmann.com

puncherandwattmann@bigpond.com

National Library of Australia
Cataloguing-in-Publication entry:

Watson, John

Triptych: Collected Works Volume 7

ISBN     9781922186997

NATIONAL
LIBRARY
OF AUSTRALIA

A catalogue record for this book is available from the National Library of Australia

Cover design by Sophie Gaur

Printed by Lightning Source International

This project has been assisted by the Australian Government through the Australia Council, its arts funding and advisory body.

Australian Government

Australia Council
for the Arts

# Contents

# 1

Improvisations on Poems from the French

# Vincent Voiture (1598-1648): To a Young Lady Who Wore the Sleeves of her Chemise Pushed Back and Soiled

You who keep unceasingly
A hundred lovers up your sleeve,
At least ensure their probity
And try to keep your sleeve less soiled.

You have the privilege to invoke
The victor's rights and justly lock
Your suitors in this prison cell,
But does it have to be so dark?

My heart, which is at your command
And which you have refused to ask,
You keep in dungeons underground
Like prisoners waiting to be hanged.

Can it be that night and day
On fire, the smouldering of my love
Has filled this place with acrid smoke
And made a chimney of your sleeve?

# Two Faltering Sonnets on the Model of the Unfinished Sonnet of Antoine-Girard de Saint-Amant (1594-1661)[1]

I'm clambering round a lumber room, a place
Where furniture is stored from former lives
Like bad King Henry's inventory of wives.
I'm writing with a candle stub on glass.

One window gives upon a fountain rill
With follies, bridge, drained fields and gilded tent;
A mirror darkly shines in puzzlement
With what must be this very pastoral.

This sonnet, like Ariadne's thread, unwinds;
The room is thunderous behind its blinds,
While afternoon goes on and on for months.

These lines must falter here. If anyone
Can find the rhyme, he's welcome to their sun ...

---

1 "We have no rhymes in English for *warmth, month, wolf, gulf, sylph, breadth, width, depth, scarce, wasp, pint, rhythm, bilge, film.*" Swann and Sidgwick, *The Making of English Verse*; see also Roy Fuller, *Tiny Tears* p64.

Peruked, pomaded, powdered like the moon,
I'm dancing with my well-feigned nonchalance;
The curtained room is turning with the dance
As I embrace my charming Columbine.

In masks we circle others masked, so that
One could almost be dancing with oneself
(At least that way one's not left on the shelf)
And all the while along my cuff I write

A sonnet which will soon reveal its lack.
I'm tapping out its measures on her back
Like Goethe's famous check on strophic rhythm.

By midnight I will know my Muse. I'll pause.
Then someone who can rhyme may seize the prize ...

# Antoine-Girard de Saint-Amant: Dirge on the Death of Silvia

Stream, hastening to pursue yourself
And fleeing from yourself also,
Halt in midstream
And for a brief
And heavy moment entertain my grief
Which having heard, resume,
To tell the sea its bitterness
Is nothing now compared to this.

Relate how Silvia, singular
And sole fair guardian of my fate,
Has met the blows
Of cruel Death,
Which plucked the unfolding flower of her breath.
Say these calamities
Have in one cataclysmic day
Invaded Love's own armoury.

Alas! I cannot voice this loss;
My sighs cut short their reverie.
Pale stream, farewell!
Once more flow on.
Your course knows no more rest than I have known.
If I have stayed this pool,
If you have slowed to hear my cries
Then let me hasten you with tears.

# Mellin de Saint-Gelais (1491-1558) : Sonnet

There are in Venice not so many boats,
Nor dappled shimmering wakes between them all,
Nor balconies which seem about to fall
Above those tides; nor swans in English moats;

Nor Savoy bears; nor calves in Brittany,
Nor haughtiness in Spain; nor lovers brought
To church; nor rank duplicities at court;
Nor arguments in all of Germany;

Nor so many monsters found in Africa;
Nor avaricious lawyers; nor, by far,
So many dreams dreamed in an abbot's bed;

Nor feast day pardons in the Vatican;
Nor disputations heard at the Sorbonne —
As my beloved has whims in her head.

# Vincent Voiture : For Madame d'Aiguillon

"The earth ablaze with flowers
Shines like painted Hours
Previously unknown.
The day-star seems to cast
Across the soft cloud throne
The azure gold with which it paints the East.

Sapphires line the sky;
The fragrant zephyrs sigh
More gently than before.
Flushed roses stain the dawn;
The day turns to adore
A light more gently beautiful than the sun.

The sweetly singing birds
Wage amorous wars of words
In concert in the glade.
Perhaps the pantheon
Of gods visits our shade,
Or in our midst moves Oronte the Divine,

She whose conquering eyes
Induce a thousand sighs
Which meet with her disdain,
She on whose illustrious birth
Heaven brightly shone
Bestowing favours from both gods and earth.

And in her luminous power
Those ancient trunks, this bower,
These forests, feel the flame
Of love.  And all is one
In her transforming charm
Whose glance creates a heart in this very stone."

So, leaving Fontenay
Along the Gourmay way
Composing verse at will
According to his mood,
Voiture, that frigid fool,
Praised love as if he felt each ardent word.

The nymphs of wood and stream
Hearing each doleful claim
Could not forebear to smile.
And yet a listening faun
Said to a dryad, "Girl!
Perhaps there's *some* truth in this unctuous man."

# Louise Labé (1524-1566) : Sonnet

Kiss me again and kiss again and still
Allow me one your most delicious ones
And then another of your amorous ones
And I'll reply with four as hot as coal.

There, does it pain? Then let me soothe these blows
By giving you a dozen, sweet and chaste,
And with their mingling in our blissful haste
Let us enjoy each other at our ease.

So then a double life for each ensues,
Each for himself and in the other's gaze,
And Love bestows this knowledge in its charms:

I am always distracted when alone
And find my true contentment only when
I venture from myself into your arms.

# Pierre de Ronsard (1524-1585) : Ode

Many from their bodies flown
Have seen themselves in distant lands
Transformed, like texts in many hands —
One to a serpent, one to stone,

Another to a startled lake,
Or wolf, or pigeon clattering away,
Or one to a flower, one a tree
Or swallow darting by a brook.

But I would like to be the glass
In which you gazed (thus gazing at me);
Or your chemise, that frequently
You'd take me up and slowly dress.

Or were I water, happily
To wash your body — how I'd toil.
Or be the perfume with whose oil
I would anoint its ivory.

I'd like to volunteer to be
The ribbon at your dazzling breast
Or else the charm in its sweet rest
Below your faultless throat.  But no —

Of all such Possibility
I'd choose to be the coral tint
Which paints your lips, without restraint
I'd kiss your mouth repeatedly.

# Jean-Baptiste Chassignet (c1570-c1635) : A Mirror

Direct a mirror to the skies
And azure skies appear to pass;
Return it to the earth or seas
And see at once that heaving mass.

Such is the force of love's fierce fire:
The heart tormented by its flame
Transforms itself to its desire,
Identical in all but name.

To love the heavens will entail
That one become celestial
While earth returns one to its world.

Thus Nebuchadnezzar, loving the earth
Too well, was made to graze a path
For seven years as beast of the field.

# Pierre de Ronsard :
# Epitaph on François Rabelais

If from a dead man Nature brings
Renewal, if from this corrupt,
Dissolving substance something apt
Is soon to be engendered here,
Then let it be a vine which springs
From the stomach (vast, capacious sphere)
Of Rabelais, who drank as if
The world were sinking under wine.
    The mine-shaft of his gaping maw
Had seen more wine pass, quaffing down
(Nose-snorted in a double stream),
Than pigs drink sweet milk from a trough,
Or Iris carried water from
The Styx when gods grew heated, or
Upsurging waves their banks consume.
    The sun could not rise soon enough
To see him not yet drinking. Nor
Could night-watch ever grow so late
To find him finished drinking. For
His thirst went on without respite;
Good Rabelais drank day and night.
    And when the ardent Dog-star burned,
Half-naked with his sleeve upturned
He'd find a quiet place to sprawl
Beneath the tankards on the wall
And, slumped amongst the greasy plates,
Stretch out and feel no shame at all.
He'd burble in his cups, take notes
And rumble like a frog in mud.

Then somewhat drunk he'd shout the praise
Of Bacchus, only friend and lord,
Under whose famous auspices
The Thebans had been overcome;
And then he'd tell how Semele
(The mother of this prodigy)
Had been a little over-warm
With Jupiter, who, in his turn,
Forgot that thunderbolts can burn
And cooked her to a crisp.

                                His grasp
Of glass and narrative alike
Were never bettered.  Dazzling work!
He sang the mare Gargantuan,
Great Panurge, and the Papimane,
Their burgeoning lives at work and play,
And Friar Jean des Antoumeures,
And the battles of Epistemon;
But Death who does not drink at all
Has dragged the drinker from this sphere
And forces him at last to swill
The muddy depths of Acheron.

              Now, passer-by, be thoughtful, brave:
Set cups of wine upon his grave
And ample flagons, saveloy,
And ham, and cheeses from the south.
For, if his soul beneath the earth
Is still the soul of Rabelais,
He'd rather these than some bouquet.

# Two Anonymous Ballads

On the steps of the palace
On the palace steps
Sits a pretty Flemish girl, O!
A pretty girl from Flanders.

She has so many suitors
So many suitors suit her
She cannot tell which to take, O!
Or know which one would please her.

One is a baker,
He is a baker of sweet breads.
Another is a manservant, Ah!
A fine lady's footman.

A little shoemaker caught her eye;
Her eye fell upon a shoemaker.
On him her choice fell. Yes!
She liked a shoemaker above all.

He will make her supple shoes,
Soft shoes are to be made for her
From Dutch morocco leather, Ah!
From the finest leather in Holland.

While putting on her shoes
And holding her foot in his hand
He made his proposal, O!
Proposing as follows:

"Fair maid, if you wish,
If it pleases you, fair maid,
We would sleep together. O!
We would sleep together.

In a big square bed
In a bed with equal sides
With white pillow covers, Yes!
With pillows like plumped clouds.

And at its four corners,
At its corners like harbours
There are bunches of periwinkle, Ah!
Blue periwinkle in bunches.

In the middle of the bed
In the middle of the bed
The river is deep. O!
The river runs deep and wide.

All the king's horses
All the horses of the royal stables
Could come to drink there, O!
Be led to water and made to drink.

And there we would sleep,
Sleep would beguile us
Until the end of the world, O!
Until the beginning of the next."

The daughter of the King of France
Is marrying the English King.
"O brothers dear, don't let this throng
        Take me away;
I'd rather a soldier from Marseilles
Than marry an English King."

And when it came to the wedding day,
She saw the whole of Paris frown.
There wasn't a lady in that town
        Who didn't weep
To see their favourite cringe and creep
Towards this English drone.

And when it came to sailing away
He offers a blindfold for her eyes.
"Blindfold yourself," she says and sighs.
        "If I must go
Across the sea, bound by my vow,
I'll look upon the seas."

And when it came to going ashore
The English drums and fiddles shrill.
"Leave off this English drumming drill;
        I want to hear
One sound alone that thrills the ear:
The French King's woodwinds trill."

And when it came to evening fare
He took his knife to cut her bread.
"Cut only for yourself," she said,
      "And not for me;
Cursed Englishman, I've lost, you see,
All appetite for food."

And when it came to going to bed,
The English King removed her shoes.
"Take off your own, but let me choose
      To be undressed
By ladies from my native coast.
I'll not pay English dues."

But when it came to midnight's bell,
The lady was unsleeping still.
"Turn round, embrace me well,
      My Englishman.
Since God has joined us, if we can,
We must obey his will."

# Antoine Girard de Saint-Amant : The Indolent

By sloth and melancholy overcome,
Dreaming, in bed, in tousled sheets I lie
Still as a boned hare sleeping in a pie
Or like Don Quixote in his manic gloom.

There, worrying not a whit about the wars
In Italy, or the old Count Palatine,
Or all his royal hangers-on, I plan
My hymn to idleness. And so I laze

And find this pleasure so serenely sweet
Sleep must confer the good life while you wait,
For already I've grown fat with idleness.

Work so appals me I close out the view;
With one hand out, my dear Badouin, I scarce
Can bring myself to write these lines for you.

# Clement Marot (1496-1544) : Rondeau

Kissing her mouth I heard her say,
"Sweet, let this fragrant kiss defray
Our long-awaited future bliss."
Her voice was gentle, as if this
Should all my rising flames allay.

But by this reckless, warm assay
She made those flames run more astray
While I stood, perfumed by her voice,
Kissing her mouth.

My spirit thrived as if it lay
Upon her lips. Then, held in sway,
Briefly she died in love's embrace.
And, had her breath stayed at my face,
I should have lost my soul this way,
Kissing her mouth.

# 2

Benjamin Constant and Germaine de Staël :
14 Rondeaux

# In the Carriage

Pursuing her on horseback he
Outrode her carriage, furiously
Reined in his mount and there began,
Beside the lake road to Lausanne
Where clouds glowed like a ruffled sea,

His sentence:  he was now to be
For fifteen years in purgatory
A prisoner of love, a man
Pursuing her,

Unable to escape.  When she
Leaned from her carriage smilingly,
Her voice burned like a cloudless sun.
He fell into the role of one
Acknowledging complicity,
Pursuing her.

# Seething Harm

Germaine de Staël invited him
To share her carriage. Soon her charm,
That freely multiplying cell,
Enveloped him. Reaching a hill
The carriage slowed. The day was calm

But everywhere behind the warm
Autumnal air lay seething harm,
Like insects hidden in a wall.
Germaine de Staël

Invited him to share her room
With curtains on the lake, the bloom
Of conversation in her pale.
He found himself in dazzling thrall,
Repeating endlessly the name
Germaine de Staël.

# Conflagration

Delicious light began to break
From sombre clouds; above the lake
Some miles away the shaken page
Of autumn lightning's muted rage
Implied the friction they would make.

Benjamin Constant at the stake
Of passion's conflagration spoke
Of vain delusions of the age.
Delicious light

Appeared to linger for her sake
Discovering always in its smoke
Habitual décolletage
In one perpetually on stage;
Her voice continued to evoke
Delicious light.

# The Journey

*And what strange pasts lie still unveiled?*
*Is love by love always reviled?*
*What are the origins of despair?*
*In what do deities inhere?*
Lost in such matters they beguiled

The journey while, outside, the world
Seemed trivial and remote; it paled
With fading lake and autumn's glare
And what strange pasts!

The carriage passed a linden wold.
In conversation now misled
They cut adrift all rescue there.
The future glowed. This much was clear:
Fresh revelations would unfold,
And what strange pasts!

# Facts

She always loved her father best.
He mourned always the mother lost
At his expulsion to the world.
Her hands were two white flags unfurled,
As if by storm or tempest tossed,

To accompany every complex jest
But never in surrender. Lust
Involved profound ideas recalled.
She always loved.

He would have changed even the past.
He favoured Feelings at all cost.
Emotion stirred in them then spilled.
They met and every time recoiled.
Those men who acted in her cast
She always loved.

# Desire

From the first she seemed to say,
*I bring these riches, that you may*
*Traverse the boundaries at will*
*Of mind and body, vale and hill*
*Of woman's multiplicity;*

*I offer here the mystery*
*Of incarnation, rapt display,*
*The mind made roundly tangible*
*From the first.*

He too was party to this play
Of dialogue between these two
Extremes: how richly visible
The splendours of the physical
Which he embraced in her and knew
From the first.

# Possession

Limpid frescoes drenched in dew,
Long melting vistas like the view
Of lake mist, curtained, sheet on sheet
Ascending through the morning's heat —
All these the smile of reason knew

And with them every voiced idea
Which discourse conjured in the air
Made of their shared voluptuous thought
Limpid frescoes.

For, just as limbs entwine, so too
Does thought with thought conjoin anew
Until at last possessive, mute
And stubborn forces breed dispute,
And what was once bright fades to mere
Limpid frescoes.

# Resonance

So dominant in all the roles
She took in their theatricals,
She played satyr and libertine
Rather than nymph; then Benjamin
Would watch, seduced by subtle wiles

And forcefulness beneath the veils.
But soon their dialectic pales,
For with the birth of Albertine,
So dominant

In their contentment, she instils
A temporary calm like lulling sails.
Echoes of Albertine remain.
They could not know that, centuries on,
The name would be, in memory's aisles,
So dominant.

# Chronology

The very year that Albertine
Was born (with hair like splashing wine
Confirming her paternity)
— A time of brief serenity —
Germaine had met Napoleon.

The time would not be long serene;
Already arguments began
And dark possessive secrecy.
That very year

United them in fierce disdain.
The publication of Corinne
Would earn Napoleon's enmity
And her own exile.  Famously
She would not banish Benjamin
For fifteen years.

# From His Memoirs

Once, in her hand, I saw the white
Of sea birds caught in winter light;
Her features rather over-large;
Perpetual décolletage;
Eyes fiercely, furiously bright.

Her mind, far-ranging, soared in flight,
Embodying more grace and wit
Than any in our stellar age.
Once, in her hands,

The entire salon gave a shout
Of approbation at her sleight;
Her charm would stay the turning page;
Her gaiety dispelled my rage;
Fate had me seeking out her heart,
Once in her hands.

# A Repeat Performance

The suicide was well rehearsed
He had in fact performed it first
To end a compromising scene
Where mother vied with daughter. (Then
He'd swallowed opium, felt its frost

And fallen — but revived at last
In time to see the pair impressed
And take the daughter to Racine.)
That suicide,

Stage-managed with a sterling cast
Now seemed to beckon from the past;
Alone, surrounded at Lausanne
By rival lovers of Germaine,
He needed to become again
The suicide.

# The Elixir of Love

He raised and quaffed the opiate,
Which was, of course, safely dilute.
He lay in restful, slumbering ease,
Then felt maternal, opulent tears
And rousing forearms' pleasant heat.

The world seemed bathed in milky light;
Her voice rang through a star-filled night:
Live, my dear Constant, hear my pleas.
Raised up, he quaffed.

She now dispensed a draught both sweet
And infinitely more fatal, yet
Unknown in his pharmacopeias:
The passion to enslave the years.
He sighed, prepared to take it straight;
He rose and quaffed.

# Divided Affections

For fifteen years a willing slave;
For fifteen years in hopeless love
With Juliette Récamier
So like a gentle summer's day,
Her beauty sweet as it is grave,

Unlike the steel hand in the glove
Who shakes me through her brilliant sieve
And has cast on my shadowy way,
For fifteen years,

Olympian lightning from above.
Between these two ideals I strive.
Now see her gazing in the way
David  has pictured her in flower!
O, had I chosen so to live
For fifteen years!

# Procession

Germaine de Staël, at her levée
Addressed her audience brilliantly:
"If Architecture is" (she sighed)
"A form of music petrified
Then let us have a library

Built on a cliff beside the sea
And let its every stone wall be
Made from the nightingale's glissade."
Germaine de Staël

Put on her turban, took up her spray
Of shrubbery and seized the day
Already well advanced. A pride
Of lovers answering every need
Raised votive palms lining the way
Of Germaine de Staël.

# 3

Galina Brezhneva: L'Amour Fou

# Rondeau

Ukrainian saltfields soapstone dull
With reeds and mournful birds.  A wall.
A girl looks out into a lane.
The circus riding into town
Is glittering diamonds.  Raptly pale,

She strokes a pony's braided tail
And  hears the clothes-line raven call:
*Look back, look back, and surely turn*
*To Ukrainian salt;*

*But follow down this sawdust trail*
*— That strongman is a lion male*
*Enormous in his pantaloon —*
*And raindrops hanging on the line*
*Are diamonds.  Seize them and reveal*
*Ukrainian salt.*

# Triple Rondel

A forest like a head of hair,
A hillside like a bosom laced
With willow wands, a snowfield crossed,

A muslin gauze of sleet-filled air —
Prefigure wedding veils to greet
*A forest like a head of hair,*
*A hillside like a bosom laced.*

A wild child runs into the snow
She has (aged five) acquired a taste
For gin and tonic. Nor must she waste
*A forest like a head of hair,*
*A hillside like a bosom laced*
*With willow wands, a snowfield crossed.*

# Rondeau prime

I want to be an actress. I could play
*Anna Karenina* of the peatmarsh plain,
But change her story: I'd seduce again
That fool, her husband. In a single day
I'd bring him to his knees. And, in a way,
I'd alter every role to suit the man
I want to be.

I'd even play a lizard — or the fly
Half crazed by aniseed that floods our lane,
Our Mars canal from crisscrossing the Ukraine …
And yet, I want more than mere fantasy,
*I want to be.*

# Carol

I take on wings.  I float, I soar,
While passion brings me to the floor.

The footlights glare, I cannot see
The audience.  And so I'm free
To improvise outrageously.
I take on wings.  I float, I soar.

I'll choose the most romantic role.
My parts are greater than the whole.
My partners pierce me to the soul
Until I hear *Encore! Encore!*

By dawn my bed becomes a throne,
And gin a tonic on its own,
And several lovers all have flown
Who might perhaps not rise to more.

To live in this star-studded state —
Electric body wired for light
With switches linked to every part —
O let light flood from every shore!

An actress has a thousand lives
And I desire as many loves,
Like hearts worn on transparent sleeves,
Always impatient to adore.

Let vodka Life still freely flow.
I'm clinging to the longest straw.
I long to hear the lion's roar
Then take the splinter from its paw.

The stage is strewn with sawdust now.
The circus strongman mops his brow.
He plants a forest with his plough,
While passion brings me to the floor.

# Quatrains

Our language has peculiar force,
　　And in its accidence retains
　　Archaic features, like the plains
Perpetually renewing wheat.

The *verb* is beautiful, like men
　　Inflected by their gaze alone
　　To voice their pleasure, while the *noun*,
Like women, needs adornment from

Its prepositions linked like jewels.
　　Diminutives exuberant!
　　The metaphor sprung like a plant
Through every fissure in the earth!

And binary polarities
　　Whose features may be seen to trace
　　Each man and woman who embrace
Then separate, once more opposed!

In aspects phonological,
　　The affricates are dominant —
　　The breath-stream stops and must supplant
The fricatives till breath returns;

In this they are like heart stops — when
　　We catch the beauty of a face
　　Or tumblers on a circus horse
Which canters in its billowing tent.

Ancient Slavic languages,
    Like meadows flowering every year,
    Return to earth then reappear
Like diamonds thrown up by the plough.

# Sonnet

You frown, dear father, and would have me join
The Youth League. But I am too fond
Of Boris (and Alexis and Yvain).
Their skin is brown like Kharkov's fertile ground,

Their thighs are like the masts of Azov ships,
Their eyes as dark as peasants' woven cloth
In the Poltava region. And their lips
Are red as silk embroidery in the north,

Where one word stands for "red" and "beautiful".
I'd rather live with them in old Kieff,
Our khata built of wood and, on its wall,
Our votive shawl embroidered to the life
With scenes of love. I'd lie with them and be
Like flax which they made linen, lovingly.

# Ballade

O heavenly and lovely specimen:
Yevgeny holding to the sweating light
The tangle of a dozen floating men
Of which just one would weigh on me like night;
And yet he lifts them all for my delight
And still has strength to burn me with his eyes.
O tree with swaying branches, each a prize,
Yet none so lovely as its base and keep,
Astride and teetering in his massive ease.
He plays upon me like a well-strung harp.

O smell of men and ore raised from a mine,
And eucalypts when summer's at its height,
And reed-logged lake, and flowering turpentine —
All blooming in this tent in torpid heat!
This living tree which staggers, flowing wet,
Has raised in me a tent of ardent sighs,
A banner I would clasp about his thighs
Proclaiming my resolve and daring hope.
His tuning hands may wander where they please
And play upon me like a well-strung harp.

O smell of thunder, roar of flowering vine,
I'm burgeoning and melting at the sight,
And sawdust everywhere must surely burn.
O let me climb this tree of men and might,
And like a blossom in its branches float,
Then die upon its strength as frenzy dies ...
And yet I faint and fear:  he must not seize

Such weights.  I want to see his face in sleep
And he have strength enough for days and days
Of playing on me like a well-strung harp.

O let me see the forest for the trees
And know the way this lofty oak to please!
Then let him come to me and shed his cape
And take me up and move through all the keys
And play upon me like a well-strung harp.

# Ballad

"My dear," the bearded lady said,
    "He's very strong.  But then,
You must by now have found his strength
    Is as the strength of ten."

When snow was falling thick as stars
    And Kharkov in its vice,
Galina ran into his clasp
    To melt like heated ice.

"It's said he's strong in every part,"
    The ballerina said,
"As much at home in circus tent
    As in a lady's bed."

*His strength is as the strength of  ten.*
    Galina thought on this:
"Pythagoras thought ten divine.
    To  me it seems like bliss."

Galina Brezhneva did not like
    The India-rubber man;
She wanted someone more like stone
    To share her caravan.

The tightrope-walker asked her up
    To share his narrow berth
But she said, "I need someone who
    Will bring me down to earth."

The fire-eater left her cold,
        The clowns seemed sadly dour,
The lion-tamer far too tame —
        But O, the oak's lithe power!

The snow was falling thick as wheat;
        The strongman raised the roof.
Auroras roared about her.  Then
        She asked no further proof.

"Galina, bear-cub dressed in furs,
        I lift you with one hand
And trail you in amongst the stars
        Above your snowbound land."

"Yevgeny, tower of strength and guide,
        Conduct me through the maze.
O corbel from your granite walls,
        Support me all my days."

# Rondel

When spring was lapped by autumn days,
Victoria, her flower, was born
While, in the Party's dark machine,
Galina's father closed his eyes

And for a year withheld his gaze.
His endless winter had begun
When spring was lapped by autumn days
And fair Victoria was born.

Then through the wheat sea's summer haze
Across the frothing, rolling plain,
The little girl was brought; and soon
Her mother left her with some sighs,
When spring was lapped by autumn days.

# Song

Rehearsing on the furrowed snows,
The acrobats are lean and fair
 And tumble me.

Exponents of the high trapeze
Embrace a moment in the air,
 Then fly with me.

The lion backs away and roars,
The lion-tamer wields his chair,
 And then wields me.

The jugglers toss those plates with ease
Which never seem to leave their care,
 Then care for me.

Yevgeny lifts a beam and stares,
He shouts of infidelities,
He drops the beam again and glares,
 But I don't care.

For Boris in his Cossack shoes,
Dimitri dancing with the bears
And Ivan with his whip and spurs —
 Each pleases me.

# Ballad

The Chairman of the Power Elite
    Stepped from the aeroplane.
His overcoat was charcoal grey,
    He wore his practised frown.

Galina had been rather loud
    As stewards flocked around;
Her dress was not the Party line
    And, as they touched the ground,

She thanked the staff for granting her
    The freedom of the air.
Then Brezhnev's frown, though permanent,
    Grew even more severe.

Zagreb by day seemed dark as night
    And suitably austere;
But in the street Galina burned,
    An incandescent flare.

That night she wore her gypsy blouse
    And dined and drank too well,
And loudly reappeared at dawn
    To tell the whole hotel

(The waiters now were all her friends)
    That she would soon be wed
And married to a conjuror
    Who conjured best in bed.

The Chairman of the Soviets
   In charcoal overcoat
Resolved that future travel plans
   Must leave his daughter out;

In fact, as Chairman of the State,
   He should always ensure
An aeroplane was standing by
   For — say — Siberia.

# Rhyme Royal

A plane was sent to bring his daughter home
From fierce Crimean vodka in the shade,
And spas and wine and Yalta's temperate warm,
To Moscow and a proper Party mood.
The conjuror was conjured from his bed,
And vanished in the waving of a wand
To be remade by Party sleight-of-hand.

While under house arrest, Galina read
And studied modern languages with zeal.
Her spirits did not noticeably fade.
As if she had not left Sevastopol,
She made her own Carpathia in her gaol.
She dressed for spring and did not draw the blinds.
She dined on caviar from Party funds.

*O ballet dancer in your leotard*
*With gas-light in your face like moonlit snow,*
*Your body is so inexplicably hard —*
*I'm floating down the Volga while you row!*
*So meet me in that whiskey bar we know;*
*We'll dance a pas de deux there in its grounds*
*With entrechats sustained beyond all bounds!*

Eyebrows were raised at the Praesidium
Each time Galina scandalised the town.
Amongst these, Brezhnev's eyebrows reigned supreme
Like two black bears stretched basking in the sun.
But something urgent needed to be done:
A husband must be found for her, and fast.
The KGB must search from coast to coast.

Now in her forties, Princess Brezhneva
Was undiminished in her energies.
If not absconding to a whiskey bar
She might be found curled up on someone's knees,
Or in his bed, or at the theatre doors.
Yury Churbanov of the KGB,
Now centre-stage, brings to this history

A marriage of convenience (although
The groom already had a family,
A minor inconvenience.) Even so,
Galina had her Moscow flat, and he
Could rise up through the ranks as Deputy
Of the Interior (where, it's true,
Uzbekistan would prove his Waterloo.)

*O Boris, Gypsy Boris, read my palm,*
*But don't stop there, my gypsy. Never cease,*
*Read all of me, proceed along my arm*
*And read my own unfolding War and Peace,*
*Or seek and you may find the Golden Fleece,*
*And tales and mysteries. Nothing is barred!*
*O Boris, be my own Sheherezade!*

# Tail-rhymes

Some orgies seemed increasingly
Exhausting.  Boris seemed to be
            Less interested in her.

The steppes were very far away
And Boris was a shade *distrait*.
            She felt strangely aware

Of body weight, mortality
And memories of the Azov Sea,
            And something close to fear.

She longed for sleep in someone's arms
But often woke alone.  Alarms
            And sorrows troubled her.

Some diamonds which she'd hoped to get
Had somehow fallen through the net
            In Transcarpathia.

When Boris too was over-free
With a lion-tamer's jewellery
            And kept the lion's share,

Her days with him were stolen too.
Soon only alcohol would do,
            Drowning each sullen care.

# Couplets

"What spirits have we here?  And what's the blend?
And cigarettes?  Américain?  I'll bend
Your ear with memories of circuses,
Spring in Odessa or the Caucasus,
And three-a-bed, and candles burning low
At both ends in those days of dazzling snow
Which fell as palaces already formed.  Where now
Are Lesya and Michail and all those Borises?
And ever-strong Yevgeny of the burning eyes?
— They say he's lifting daffodils in Kursk ...
These bottles are all drained.  You've brought a cask?
Then I'll go on.  It is our fate at last
— And mine exceedingly more dire than most —
To turn into our fathers.  Nonetheless
— Please interrupt me if I've mentioned this —
I married recently.  This is a fourth
And final fling.  The orange blossom path
Leads me again to bridal happiness.
I gave up alcohol for love and — may I stress
That I was sixty-five, he twenty-nine
And, if not oak or elm, a useful pine
Like those young saplings in the Central steppes
Or those on Mt Hoverla and its slopes
In summer with the circus.  Ah, the tent
And smell of bitumen everywhere we went!
And lying down in fields like flowering snow
And being held at evening's after-glow
By strong men's arms.  But that was long ago.
I thank you.  Yes.  No water.  Gorbachev?
The mark of Cain!  But still I cling to love,

And love's the cure for all this body weight
And alcohol and diamonds and the flight
Of all the sawdust past.  But fill my glass …"